Published in 2013 by The Rosen Publishing Group, Inc.
29 East 21st Street, New York, NY 10010

Photo Credits: **KEY** tl=top left; tc=top center; tr=top right; cl=center left; c=center; cr=center right; bl=bottom left; bc=bottom center; br=bottom right; bg=background

BM = British Museum; CBT = Corbis; GI = Getty Images; iS = istockphoto.com; NGS = National Geographic Society; SH = Shutterstock; TPL = photolibrary.com; wiki = Wikipedia

front cover GI; **4**c iS; **4–5**bc NGS; **6**bc iS; **8**cl iS; **9**tr iS; **10**bl, c iS; **11**tr iS; **12**bc GI; bl TPL; **15**br GI; br, tr iS; **18**br GI; **18–19**tc GI; **19**c TPL; **20**bc, br CBT; bl, br, tr iS; tr NGS; **21**cr CBT; bc, bl, br, cl, tl, tr iS; bc TPL; **22**tl CBT; **22–23**cr CBT; **28**tc BM; cr GI; bl, br, tl iS; bl TPL; **29**cr CBT; bc, bc, bl GI; cr, tl iS; cl NGS; br SH; tr wiki; **32**bg iS

All illustrations copyright Weldon Owen Pty Ltd

Weldon Owen Pty Ltd
Managing Director: Kay Scarlett
Creative Director: Sue Burk
Publisher: Helen Bateman
Senior Vice President, International Sales: Stuart Laurence
Vice President Sales North America: Ellen Towell
Administration Manager, International Sales: Kristine Ravn

Library of Congress Cataloging-in-Publication Data

Stephens, David R., 1945-
 Treasure hunters / by David Stephens.
     p. cm. — (Discovery education: sensational true stories)
 Includes index.
 ISBN 978-1-4777-0058-7 (library binding) — ISBN 978-1-4777-0101-0 (pbk.) —
 ISBN 978-1-4777-0102-7 (6-pack)
 1. Treasure trove—Juvenile literature. I. Title.
 G525.S88133 2013
 622'.19—dc23
                              2012019802

Manufactured in the United States of America

CPSIA Compliance Information: Batch #W13PK2: For Further Information contact Rosen Publishing, New York, New York at 1-800-237-9932

SENSATIONAL TRUE STORIES

TREASURE HUNTERS

DAVID STEPHENS

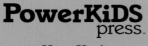

PowerKiDS press.

New York

Contents

What Is Treasure?

Treasure can be anything that is rare or unique. It could be an old book that once sold for a dime. If that book is now the only one left of its kind, it is priceless. Treasure can be a rare comic, an unusual stamp, or an antique toy. Most homes have at least one item of treasure somewhere under the roof. If you have something that cannot be replaced easily, it is probably treasure.

Before banks existed, people kept their wealth in a wooden box or chest. This was handy if you needed cash quickly, but it was also easy for others to steal. When traveling overseas, people took their treasure chest with them, perhaps containing fine jewelry, gold coins, and valuable personal items that they used to emphasize their wealth and power. But it was not very convenient or safe. If the ship was caught in a storm and sank, you might save yourself, but the chest would go to the bottom with the ship.

WHY IS GOLD SO VALUABLE?

Gold is rare and difficult to mine. To extract 1 ounce (28 g) of gold from the ground, at least 10 tons (9 t) of rock must be moved. Gold is prized for jewelry making because it is soft and easy to shape. It does not tarnish or corrode. This makes it useful for electrical connectors in computers and other electrical equipment.

Gold ingots

Jeweled crown
The royal families of the world possess many items of treasure. This crown was made for King James V of Scotland in 1540.

Tiara
Mixed gemstones are set in a gold tiara, which was probably worn for special occasions by a member of a royal family.

Treasure chest

In the fifteenth century, the Spanish shipped gold and silver coins around the world in large wooden chests. These chests were probably the origin of the term treasure chest.

Coins
Around the sixth century BC, the first coins were made of a gold and silver alloy found naturally in the rivers of western Turkey.

Gold goblet
Royal and noble families had plates, cups, and knives made of pure gold as a sign of their position in the community.

World currency
The first coins used as world currency were called pieces of eight. They were minted by the Spanish from the fifteenth century.

California Gold Rush

I n January 1848, James Marshall discovered gold in the American River at Coloma, California. He was building a sawmill for his employer, Captain John Sutter, at the time, and he noticed flakes of gold in the water from the millrace, a canal used to drive the mill wheel. Despite Marshall trying to keep his discovery a secret, news spread quickly around the United States and then overseas. By 1849, the California Gold Rush was well underway. Over the next few years, 300,000 people traveled by ship or covered wagons to join the rush for gold and seek their fortune. Often, they suffered great hardship.

The very early gold miners were known as forty-niners, after the year 1849, which was the year when most of them arrived in California. Initially, the gold was easy to find by panning for it. This involved swirling the river mud with water in a flat pan so the heavy gold sank to the bottom. But by the mid-1800s, most of this gold had run out, leaving only deposits in rock that had to be mined.

Californian ghost towns
Towns sprang up throughout northern California to service miners. In 1880, the town of Bodie had a population of 10,000 people and a reputation for lawlessness. Today, it is a ghost town.

FOOL'S GOLD

Inexperienced miners sometimes thought they had struck it rich when they dug up a nugget of pyrite. Iron pyrite, a mixture of iron and sulfur, has a brassy yellow color and is often found in the same area as gold. Unfortunately, it is relatively worthless and became known as fool's gold.

Iron pyrite crystals

Sluicing for gold

To speed up panning for gold, water from the river was diverted down a long wooden sluice. Mud and gravel were shoveled in. The heavier gold sank to the bottom, where it was trapped against the ridges set into the bottom of the sluice. Every so often, the flow of water was stopped so miners could get the gold from the sluice.

Precious Metals

I f you know where to go looking, Earth is a treasure trove of precious metals. Deep below the ground, gold and silver are forced into cracks in rocks. Over time, volcanic activity in Earth's core pushes the rocks to the surface. Water erosion washes some of the gold and silver from the rock and, because they are heavy, they eventually find their way to the bottom of rivers. It was in riverbeds that gold and silver nuggets were first discovered by humans more than 5,000 years ago. The ancient Egyptians and Persians hammered these soft, shiny metals into beautiful jewelry and ornaments.

The metal platinum is even more rare than gold and silver, and much more valuable. It has a high melting point. So despite its high price, it is used in car exhaust systems to help remove toxic gases from exhaust fumes.

Real silver
Silver is often found with zinc, copper, and indium. The ore is crushed and processed to extract the different metals. This rare nugget of pure silver was found in Canada.

Ancient Greek coins
These silver coins date back to the sixth century BC. They have been stamped by hand with the images of Greek gods and mythical animals.

Platinum

Platinum nuggets are usually very tiny, no larger than a pea. The Spanish found platinum in the Americas during the seventeenth century. They called it *platina,* meaning "little silver," because they did not think it was very valuable. Platinum jewelry is popular in the United States and Japan. It is sometimes mistakenly called white gold, which is an alloy of gold and another metal.

Platinum nugget

Platinum ring

Gold nuggets

Finding gold nuggets this big is rare. These are copies of two nuggets found in 1870 in Australia. The real, original nuggets weighed 1,114 ounces (31,581 g) and 912 ounces (25,855 g) and would be too heavy to carry.

Treasures for the Afterlife

Finding buried treasure takes time and persistence. Howard Carter, an archaeologist funded by an English nobleman, Lord Carnarvon, searched the Valley of the Kings in Egypt for five years before finding the entrance to Tutankhamen's tomb. During excavations on the morning of November 4, 1922, a water boy discovered an unusual rock that turned out to be the top stair of a flight leading down to the sealed door of a tomb.

The tomb was that of Tutankhamen, a boy king of Egypt who died in 1323 BC at 19 years old. It was filled with magnificent golden treasures, including furniture, clothes, jewelry, ornaments, weapons, and even chariots, that might help him in the afterlife. The tomb consisted of four chambers, one of which contained the remains of Tutankhamen in a coffin made of solid gold.

Death mask of Tutankhamen
The death mask has colored glass and semiprecious stones set in gold. The vulture and cobra on the forehead were symbols that gave divine protection.

Antechamber
Life-size statues of Tutankhamen guarded the entrance to the burial chamber on the west wall of the antechamber.

A pharaoh's tomb
Tutankhamen's tomb consisted of four rooms reached by a passageway. It contained more than 3,500 different items, most of which are now in the Egyptian Museum in Cairo.

The head of Tutankhamen
The linen-wrapped head of the mummified Tutankhamen is displayed in a protective glass case inside his tomb at Luxor, in the Valley of the Kings.

Treasury
The treasury had a collection of model boats and Tutankhamen's preserved organs in a beautifully carved block of translucent calcite.

Annex
The annex was filled with everyday items that Tutankhamen might have used, such as games, chairs, couches, and beds.

Nested coffins
Inside a stone sarcophagus were three coffins, one inside the other. The smallest was solid gold and contained the mummified body of Tutankhamen.

Burial chamber
The burial chamber held four nested shrines, covered in gold and inscriptions to protect Tutankhamen from evil in the afterlife.

El Dorado

In the early sixteenth century, the Spanish explorers Hernán Cortés and Francisco Pizarro conquered many South American villages. They sent back vast quantities of Aztec and Inca gold to Europe, along with extravagant stories of a city made of pure gold, which they called El Dorado. Many treasure seekers have looked for this lost city of gold, but none have found it.

There is probably some truth to the legend of the city of El Dorado. Early European explorers were told of the Muisca people, who dressed their king in pure gold. He was set afloat on Lake Guatavita (which is in present-day Colombia) to make gold offerings to the Sun god, who lived in the lake.

Quest for gold

Many treasure seekers in search of El Dorado walked right past Lake Guatavita. Others, aware of the legend, planned ways to lower the water level of the lake so they could reach the gold objects. For the Indians, gold was a sacred metal, a symbol of life and fertility, not of wealth.

Lake Guatavita
In 1545, Hernán Pérez de Quesada found 40 pounds (18 kg) of gold by lowering the level of the lake by 10 feet (3 m). It took hundreds of slaves with buckets three months to do this.

The golden king
After coating their king in gold dust, the Muisca placed him on a reed raft piled high with gold and jewels. He spread these around the lake to honor the Sun god.

Feather headdress

Gold dust

Ceremonial raft
This gold model of the king's raft is now in the Gold Museum in the capital of Colombia. It was found inside a clay pot in a cave near the town of Pasca, Colombia, in 1969.

Stag's head rhyton
This beautifully crafted vessel was part of treasure found by three brothers in the Bulgarian village of Panagyurishte in 1949. They found a total of nine gold items.

Collapsible crown
This collapsible gold crown could be hidden easily. It was discovered in 1978 in a tomb in an area of Afghanistan where nomadic tribes once came to trade.

Cresent of gold
Six tombs were discovered in a part of Afghanistan near where the Silk Road had run. The tombs held 20,000 gold ornaments. This gold crescent was one of the pieces.

Treasure Hoards

Around the world, caches of treasure have been hidden by their owners, who fully intended to return and retrieve them one day. But due to unforeseen circumstances, they never did, and the treasure was discovered hundreds of years later by lucky treasure seekers. Often, these treasure troves would be found on well-traveled trade routes, such as the Silk Road.

Sometimes, treasure was buried on deserted islands, such as the treasure of Captain William Kidd, who was hanged for piracy in 1701. He tried to bribe his jailers with part of his treasure, but they did not believe him and so he died without revealing its location. He supposedly left behind four treasure maps hidden in his furniture.

Lucky find

Treasure seekers are rarely lucky enough to just trip over a hoard, but it can happen. In 1912, two boys, Valentin and Daryna Krychenko, were playing near the river Vorskla in Kiev, Ukraine. Valentin fell over in the long grass and found a huge golden pitcher filled with gold and silver.

Silver Ariadne plate

This plate is decorated with images from Greek mythology, and was part of a cache found in the walls of a Roman fort at Augusta Raurica, in Switzerland.

Sword hilt collar

Made of solid gold and inlaid with precious stones, this seventh-century Anglo-Saxon sword hilt collar was among a hoard of 1,500 weapons uncovered in Staffordshire, in England.

Mystery strip

This bent strip of gold was also part of the Staffordshire hoard. It is inscribed with verses from the Bible in Latin.

Uluburun Wreck

Discovered in 1982 off the Mediterranean coast of Turkey by a sponge diver, the *Uluburun* wreck was a 50-foot- (15 m) long wooden ship that sank in about 1306 BC. Archaeologists were excited about the cargo because it was possibly of royal origin and came from all the major trading countries of the time around the Mediterranean Sea.

The cargo contained more than 18,000 Bronze Age artifacts: from Cyprus, copper and tin ingots, the raw materials for making weapons; from Egypt and Canaan, jewelry in gold and silver; from Mycenaean Greece, spears, bronze weapons, and tools; and from Africa, elephant and hippopotamus ivory. Archaeological divers worked on the wreck for a three-month period every year for 10 years, diving to depths of 200 feet (61 m) to recover as many items as they could.

Artifacts
More than 1 ton (0.9 t) of terebinth resin, the sap from a turpentine tree used to make perfumes and incense, was found in 150 jars. It would have been traded for other items.

Recovering treasure
Divers used powerful pumps equipped with filters to remove sand from the wreck site and recover small coins and items of jewelry. Balloons filled with air were used to lift heavier items to the surface.

The original ship

This artist's impression shows how the ship *Uluburun* would have looked before centuries spent underwater rotted its timbers. This type of vessel was constructed by assembling the outer planks first, then adding the internal ribs.

Treasure Hunters

From circus strongmen to deep-sea divers, from amateur archaeologists to those who inspired the *Indiana Jones* movies—treasure hunters come from many backgrounds. Over the centuries, many treasures have been discovered on land and in the sea. Some treasure seekers have become wealthy from their finds, while some have been cursed with sickness and death, and others have been labeled thieves and robbers. They all have one thing in common—the patience and determination to research thoroughly and to keep exploring in the face of constant failure.

Jeweled cross

Sir William Phipps (1651–1695)

An American from a poor family, Phipps took a commission from the king of England to find sunken Spanish treasure ships in the Caribbean. He found 16 ships and salvaged a fortune in gold and silver. He was knighted by King James II of England and appointed the first governor of Massachusetts.

Giovanni Belzoni (1778–1824)

Italian circus strongman and engineer Belzoni became interested in archaeology after the British embassy in Egypt asked him to remove a 7-ton-(6.4 t) statue of Ramses II from a temple at Thebes, in Egypt, and ship it to the British Museum in England. He went on to discover five pharaohs' tombs in the Valley of the Kings, in Egypt.

Giovanni Belzoni

Heinrich Schliemann (1822–1890)

A millionaire and amateur archaeologist, Schliemann used his knowledge of Greek mythological stories, which he believed were based on fact, to discover archaeological sites. He proposed that the ancient city of Troy was located at Hisarlik in Turkey, which was later proved correct. He also excavated treasures at Mycenae, an ancient Greek settlement.

Gold death mask

Hiram Bingham (1875–1956)

Bingham was a professor of history and politics at Harvard University who rediscovered the lost Inca city of Machu Picchu, in Peru, in 1911. He is widely thought to be the person that the movie character Indiana Jones is based on.

Machu Picchu

Mel Fisher (1922–1998)

This scuba diving pioneer found two of the most valuable wrecks in history during exploration of the Florida Keys. The treasure he recovered from the Spanish galleon *Nuestra Señora de Atocha* included gold, silver, and copper ingots, silver coins, and emeralds.

Gold and copper ingots

Robert F. Marx (born 1933)

An American scuba diving pioneer and prolific author, Marx has worked on almost 90 shipwrecks and marine archaeological sites worldwide. He has recovered more than 200,000 artifacts from one wreck alone, that of the *Nuestra Señora de los Milagros*, which sank off the coast of Mexico in 1741.

Ancient map and coins

Edward Lee Spence (born 1947)

Spence was 12 years old when he found his first shipwreck. During a lifelong career as a treasure hunter and underwater archaeologist, he has salvaged more than $50 million worth of gold, silver, and valuable artifacts from pirate ships, Spanish galleons, and also Confederate treasure ships.

Recovered gold bullion

Ear decoration
This was worn as a type of earplug. It was made of gold and inlaid with turquoise and other semiprecious stones. The decoration shows a Moche warrior.

Sipán

Doctor Walter Alva, director of the Brüning Museum in Peru, was called out by police in the middle of the night of February 25, 1987, to identify artifacts stolen from a local archaeological site. Thieves had accidentally tunneled into the tomb of the Lord of Sipán. The Lord of Sipán was a prominent leader of the Moche people, who ruled the northern coast of Peru from about AD 1–700.

The tomb was the first of four tombs to be uncovered at Sipán, in northern Peru. This tomb contained the body of the Lord of Sipán, who died in about AD 290 at the age of 40. He was buried along with a ten-year-old child, some women—possibly his wives—and two guards, who may have been sacrificed at the time of the burial, as their feet had been cut off. There was the body of a dog to provide protection in the afterlife, and the bodies of two llamas to provide food. The tomb also contained many valuable items of gold and silver, as well as ceramic pots.

Tomb of the Lord of Sipán
Spread around the tomb were many ceramic pots that may have contained food. There were ornate tools, decorated silver and gold rattles, knives, and the bodies of a dog and two llamas.

First woman's body
This is a young woman who probably died before the Lord of Sipán and was later reburied with him. Her coffin is made of reeds.

First guard
This body is covered in copper armor. There are signs that both guards may have been sacrificed at the time of the Lord's burial.

Lord of Sipán
He was buried in full regalia: two necklaces, ear decorations made of turquoise, a gold death mask, and a scepter-like object of gold.

Second guard
This guard was placed facing the opposite way to the other guard, as if they would protect the Lord from danger in both directions.

Second woman's body
A second young woman was possibly a wife, like the other woman. Her face is covered in an ornate copper mask.

Sutton Hoo

Sutton Hoo is the site of 20 Anglo-Saxon burial mounds, known as barrows, that date back to the sixth and seventh century AD. They overlook the River Deben in Suffolk, England. The largest mound was excavated in 1939 by Basil Brown, from Ipswich Museum. He did this at the request of the person who owned the land, Edith Pretty, who supposedly had a psychic premonition that the large mound contained hidden treasure.

The excavation revealed the outline of a boat about 90 feet (27 m) long. It was the type of boat used by Anglo-Saxon mariners and would have been powered by 40 oarsmen. Further excavation uncovered a burial chamber in the center of the boat. It contained valuable items, including gold coins, gold and garnet uniform decorations, a gold buckle, two gold bars, a royal scepter, and armor complete with weapons.

Burial chamber

This chamber was 17 feet (5.5 m) long and originally covered by a wooden roof. No actual body was found because the area's acidic soil dissolves bones. However, forensic tests showed there had once been a body.

KING RAEDWALD

Archaeologists believe Sutton Hoo was the burial place of King Raedwald. He was crowned king of East Anglia and then of all England. He died in AD 624. A masked helmet found in the burial chamber was decorated in bronze.

Helmet reconstructed by archeologists

King Raedwald

Great gold buckle
The intricate patterns on this buckle matched the patterns on other clothing decorations found in the grave, including shoulder clasps and a matching purse clasp.

Royal sword
Also in the burial chamber was a rusted sword with a solid gold handle studded in garnets. Its great beauty suggests it was not used as a weapon but instead had a ceremonial purpose.

Treasure Sites

Treasure can be found just about anywhere on Earth. Gold can still be dug from abandoned mines and goldfields. And if the past is anything to go by, there are many caches of treasure, lost for generations, that are waiting to be uncovered by a determined treasure seeker. There are hundreds of shipwrecks still to be explored, some of which will become accessible only when deep-sea diving methods improve. Some legendary treasure troves may not exist at all. Their location and their very existence will turn out to be just rumors, passed down from generation to generation.

Technology is the new tool of the treasure seeker. High-definition satellite imaging, ground-penetrating radar, and unmanned drone aircraft are just a few of the tools used to locate potential treasure sites.

Fortunes lost and found

This map marks places where treasure has been found and where undiscovered treasure is supposed to lie. You could use it as the starting point for your own search for treasure.

KEY
- Treasure found
- Treasure lost

NORTH AMERICA

RMS *Titanic* (Newfoundland)

Kidd's Treasure (Gardiner's Island)

Oak Island (Nova Scotia)

Montezuma's Treasure (Utah)

Beale Ciphers (Virginia)

Lost Dutchman's Goldmine (Arizona)

SS *Central America* (North Carolina)

"Coconut" Wreck (Bermuda)

Nuestra Señora de Atocha (Florida Keys)

ATLANTIC OCEAN

Nuestra Señora de los Milagros (Mexico)

Chichén Itzá (Mexico)

Quedagh Merchant (Dominican Republic)

PACIFIC OCEAN

Treasures of Lima (Unknown Pacific island)

El Dorado (Colombia)

Machu Picchu (Peru)

SOUTH AMERICA

Spanish Loot on Crusoe Island (Juan Fernández Islands)

EUROPE

Amber Room
(Russian Federation)

ASIA

Leprechaun Gold
(Ireland)

Gundestrup Cauldron
(Denmark)

Egypt
antic)

Sutton Hoo
(England)

HMS *Victory*
(English Channel)

Panagyurishte
(Bulgaria)

Pereshchepina
(Ukraine)

Lost Tomb of
Genghis Khan
(Northwest China)

Kaiseraugst
(Switzerland)

Boscoreale
(Italy)

Elgin Marbles
(Greece)

Oxus Treasure
(Turkmenistan)

"Black Swan"
(Portugal)

"Oldest" Wreck
(Aegean Sea)

Mask of Agamemnon
(Greece)

Bactrian Hoard
(Afghanistan)

*Nuestra Señora
de la Concepción*
(Northern Mariana Islands)

Tutankhamen
(Egypt)

TROPIC OF CANCER

"Young Memnon"
(Egypt)

AFRICA

King Solomon's Mines
(Yemen)

Ark of the Covenant
(Ethopia)

Pirate Queen's Domain
(South China Sea)

EQUATOR

Lost Island
of Irisiyawa
(Indian Ocean)

Belitung Wreck
(Java Sea)

*INDIAN
OCEAN*

TROPIC OF CAPRICORN

AUSTRALIA

TauTona Mine
(South Africa)

Hand of Faith
(Australia)

Treasure Facts

Buried treasure

As they advanced across Europe, Roman armies gathered treasure as part of the spoils of war. When they were recalled to Rome, soldiers and officials buried whatever they could not carry with them to hide it from rival armies. One of the richest buried treasures was discovered by accident in Hoxne, Suffolk, England in 1992. The treasure was thought to be buried around the fifth century and, along with coins, contained all kinds of precious objects.

Silver statue of a tigress found at Hoxne

Gold coins

Gold tokens were used as gifts by the Egyptians as far back as 2700 BC. The first gold coins used throughout Europe were Celtic coins. These were produced between 54 BC and AD 43 and were literally worth their weight in gold. In the early twentieth century, gold was no longer used for currency except for limited edition coins.

Celtic gold coins

Crystal skull from the Trocadero Museum in Paris

Fictitious treasure

The film *Indiana Jones and the Kingdom of the Crystal Skull* is loosely based on fact. Real crystal skulls, supposedly found in South America, do exist in museums throughout the world but are now considered to be forgeries.

Most revealing shipwreck

The *Belitung* wreck is an Arab dhow dating from the seventh century BC. Found in the Java Sea, it revealed the existence of a lucrative, ancient ocean trade route between China and Arabia, equivalent to the famous "Silk Road," the land route across Asia.

Dragonhead jar from the *Belitung* shipwreck

Early Hellenic-style pottery like this was found at the Dokos shipwreck site.

Oldest known shipwreck

Around 2500 BC, a wooden ship sank in the Aegean Sea near Dokos, an island east of the Peloponnese. The ship has long since disintegrated, but hundreds of clay vases and other ceramic vessels remain on the seabed, marking the site of this very old wreck.

NATURE'S TREASURES

Natural processes deep within Earth create valuable gems. Diamonds form under extreme pressure deep inside Earth's mantle, then float up to the crust with volcanic magma flows. They are the hardest natural mineral and therefore the most valuable. Sapphires are found naturally underground, but can be made synthetically. The first known emerald mines belonged to the Egyptian queen Cleopatra. Opals are made from layers of crystalline silica and are mined mostly in Australian deserts. These days, gold nuggets, although they can still be panned from rivers, are mostly mined from the ground.

Opals

Diamond

Sapphire

Gold

Emerald

Glossary

archaeological diver (ar-kee-uh-LA-jih-kul DY-ver) An underwater diver who specializes in exploring the past.

archaeologist (ahr-kee-AH-luh-jist) Someone who studies the culture of ancient people by excavating sites to search for human and material remains.

Ariadne (ah-ree-AD-nee) A character from Greek mythology who was the daughter of King Minos of Crete.

artifact (AR-tih-fakt) A man-made item recovered by an archaeologist.

calcite (KAL-syt) Crystallized calcium carbonate.

Canaanite (KAY-nuh-nyt) Originating from the ancient Middle East area known as Canaan.

dhow (DOW) An Arab ship with triangular sails and one or two masts.

goblet (GOB-lit) A bowl-shaped drinking vessel.

indium (IN-dee-um) A metal element similar to aluminum.

ingot (ING-gut) A metal cast in the shape of a block for ease of handling.

iron pyrite (EYE-urn PY-ryt) A mineral of iron and sulfur also known as iron sulfide.

Moche civilization (MOH-chay sih-vih-lih-ZAY-shun) An ancient civilization that ruled northern Peru around AD 100–700.

Mycenaean (my-suh-NEE-un) Describes an ancient civilization that existed in Greece from around the sixteenth to the twelfth century BC.

panning (PAN-ing)
A method of retrieving gold
from river mud.

pharaoh (FER-oh) A leader of
ancient Egypt.

pieces of eight
(PEES-es UV AYT) Spanish silver
coins minted in the fifteenth
century. One piece was worth
eight reales.

platinum (PLAT-num)
Heavy, precious metal that
is white-gray in color.

rhyton (RY-ton) A drinking
vessel, often in the shape of an
animal's head.

sarcophagus
(sar-KAH-fuh-gus)
A coffin, usually carved from
stone or wood.

sluice (SLOOS) A manmade
channel of water.

tiara (tee-AH-ruh) A woman's
headdress that is similar to a
small crown and often jeweled.

treasure (TREH-zher)
Stored wealth, usually in the
form of money or jewels, and
sometimes very rare items.

Tutankhamen
(too-tan-KAH-men) A pharaoh,
or leader of Egypt, who ruled
between the period 1333 and
1324 BC.

Index

Websites

Due to the changing nature of Internet links, PowerKids Press has developed an online list of websites related to the subject of this book. This site is updated regularly. Please use this link to access the list:
www.powerkidslinks.com/disc/thunt/